·A·D·V·E·R·T·I·S·I·N·G·

David Lusted

Points of View

Abortion
Advertising
Alcohol
Animal Rights
Censorship
Crime and Punishment
Divorce
Drugs

Medical Ethics
Northern Ireland
Nuclear Weapons
Pollution
Racism
Sex and Sexuality
Smoking
Terrorism

Acknowledgements

The Publishers have attempted to contact all copyright holders of the quotations in this title, and apologize if there have been any oversights.

The Publishers gratefully acknowledge permission from the following to reproduce copyright material: Angus & Robertson for an extract from *Billboard Art* (1981) by Sally Henderson and Robert Landau; Associated Business Press for an extract from *The Business of Advertising* (1979) by David Farbey; Boston Press for an extract from *The Nervous Housewife* (1929) by Abraham Myerson; Century Hutchinson for two extracts from *British Television Advertising: The First 30 Years* (1986), edited by Brian Henry; Comedia for two extracts from *Understains* (1986) by Kathy Myers and for an extract from *Teaching the Media* (1985) by Len Masterman; Heinemann for an extract from *Advertising* (1982) by Frank Jefkins; Hilary Shipman for two extracts from *Television is Good for Your Kids* (1989) by Maire Messenger Davies; Macmillan for an extract from *The Complete Guide to Advertising* (1984) by Torin Douglas; McGraw-Hill for an extract from *Captains of Consciousness; Advertising and the Social Roots of the Consumer Culture* (1976) by Stuart Ewen; Methuen for two extracts from *Advertising as Communication* (1982) by Gillian Dyer; Pandora Press for three extracts from *Pictures of Women* (1984) by Jane Root; Pelican for an extract from *Discrimination and Popular Culture* (1964) edited by Denys Thompson and for an extract from *Ways of Seeing* (1976) by John Berger; Penguin for two extracts from *The Shocking History of Advertising* (1952) by E S Turner; Routledge & Kegan Paul for two extracts from *Spray it Loud* (1982) by Jill Posner.

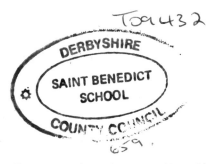

Front cover: *A contemporary artist provides one view of advertising.*

Editor: Janet De Saulles
Designer: David Armitage

First published in 1991 by
Wayland (Publishers) Limited
61 Western Road, Hove
East Sussex BN3 1JD, England

© Copyright 1991 Wayland (Publishers) Limited

British Library Cataloguing in Publication Data
Lusted, David
 Advertising. – (Points of view)
 1. Advertising — Sociological perspectives
 1. Title   11. Series
 302.23
ISBN 0-7502-0002-2

Phototypeset by Direct Image Photosetting Ltd,
Hove, East Sussex, England.
Printed in Italy by G. Canale & C.S.pA, Turin
Bound in France by A.G.M.

Contents

Introduction

Advertising is the process of drawing attention to something which is for sale. Manufacturers advertise their goods or services while organizations advertise themselves and their ideas.

As long as human society has been around, there has been some form of advertising, however basic. The advertising industry, however, is more recent, dating from around the middle of the nineteenth century. It is from this time that advertising becomes central to the economies of industrial nations; that is, central to making profit from manufacturing and selling goods. It is from this time too that serious attention is given to the nature and effects of advertising on economics, the mass media and contemporary society.

Levi's have achieved massive sales with their popular adverts: here, Eddie Kidd models jeans and jacket.

WHY WAIT TILL
YOUR HOMECOMING TO FEEL
RIGHT AT HOME.

You can't beat American know-how.

Steaks? They're just the way you like 'em. Cooked to a T.

The coffee is our own special blend, and it keeps on coming.

Films are called movies. Biscuits are called cookies. And service is spelt s-m-i-l-e.

In short, from the moment you board, the welcome is sunny side up.

Something else you'll warm to: American's low military fares that give you up to 70% discount.

They apply to every one of the 119 transatlantic flights we operate each week from 13 European cities.

Flights, moreover, that can deliver you pretty much door-to-door, thanks to our network of connections serving over 230 North American cities,* one of them more than likely your own home town.

If we sound like your kind of outfit, call your nearest SATO, travel agent or American Airlines office.

We'll put out all the flags for you.

AmericanAirlines
Something special in the air.

*Some served by American Eagle, our regional airline associate.

Left *Advertising agencies are always keen to take on international clients. BMP DDB Needham, one of the largest UK agencies, handles the American Airlines account.*

Below *An attractive advert typical of the late nineteenth and early twentieth centuries.*

Cosmydor
Savon
SE VEND PARTOUT

People who argue about advertising are called critics, whether they argue for or against it. When critics argue, it is said that they are in debate, even if they do not know of the specific critics or the views they are opposing.

Over the last 100 years or so, there have been many critics of advertising. Some have been enthusiastic about it while others have been more fearful of it. Critics may promote or oppose it, but they all contribute to how it is understood today. This book introduces you to the debate about advertising, a debate that began with advertising and continues today. It will be continued with the act of you reading this book and perhaps even be developed by you as you discuss various ideas about advertising with your friends.

Right *The strong but simple image of this Benetton clothes advert creates the kind of impact advertisers constantly strive for.*

Below *Charities often use direct black and white photography to encourage people to support their activities.*

How can you enjoy your Christmas knowing what hers will be like?

The Children's Society.
Needed now more than ever.

Every country in the world has its own rules for controlling how much and what kind of advertising it will allow. The rules are intended to protect ordinary people from advertisers making false claims. This is known as consumer protection.

In Britain, complaints from the public about advertisements (or adverts, for short) are received by the Advertising Standards Authority (ASA) which goes on to advise the advertising industry accordingly. It has no legal force but adverts that the ASA complains about are generally withdrawn. Its powers and practices are typical of the many organizations like it all over the world, each organization regulating the advertising industry in its own country. The equivalent agency in the USA is the National Advertising Review Board (NARB) and in Australia, the Advertising Standards Council (ASC).

The ASA has a long list of regulations in its Code of Advertising. The main ones have been reduced to a slogan: the Code says adverts must be legal, honest, decent and truthful.

● Legal – An advert should not encourage or appear to condone illegal or criminal acts.

● Honest – An advert should not make claims which cannot be verified. Superlatives, (eg best, finest), should only be used when they are likely to be understood as obvious exaggeration. An advert should not deliberately mislead the consumer.

● Decent – An advert should not cause grave or widespread offence to the standards of decency of those likely to see it.

● Truthful – An advert should not misuse scientific research or data to make exaggerated claims for the product.

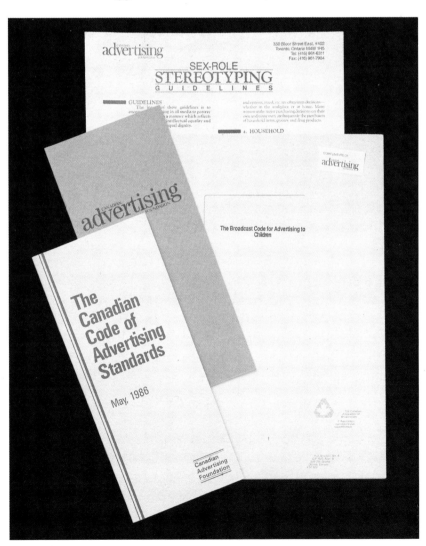

Left *The Canadian Code of Advertising Standards is set out by the Canadian Advertising Foundation.*

This may seem straightforward and reasonable but there are problems with any code. Some critics say that although almost everyone would agree about what is legal, what is honest, decent and truthful is a matter of opinion rather than law.

We can see a case in point when the ASA required the Royal Society for the Prevention of Cruelty to Animals (RSPCA) to withdraw an advert for a dog registration scheme. The ASA said that the advert was dishonest and untruthful, maintaining that the RSPCA 'claimed a direct link between the abolition of the dog licence and an increase in dog destruction' when the link was unproven.

The problem here is less that one side is right and the other wrong, but that in a matter of opinion the test of 'honesty' and 'truthfulness' cannot be applied. Nonetheless, the complaint was

This RSPCA poster had to be withdrawn when the ASA decided that the advert was misleading.

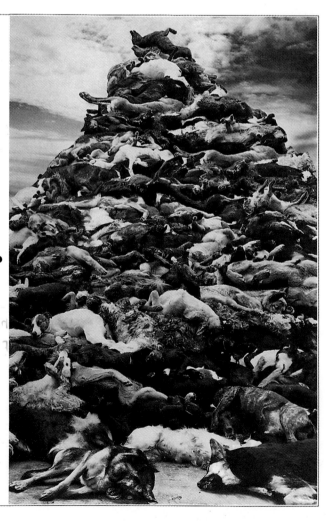

When the Government killed the dog licence they left us to kill the dogs.

One thousand dogs are killed in Britain every day.

For the most part, healthy dogs and puppies with years of life left in them.

The killings take place at local vets, in RSPCA centres and other animal charities throughout the country.

The dogs are given an overdose of anaesthetic and die within seconds.

A van makes regular collections and the dead dogs are taken to the local incinerator.

It doesn't take long to turn a Jock, Spot or Sandy into a small pile of ashes.

This daily slaughter is strange work for a society founded to prevent cruelty to animals.

We hate the killing.

We are sick of doing the Government's dirty work behind closed doors.

We want you to help us force through a dog registration scheme.

The dogs we kill are homeless dogs. Unwanted, or strays left

to roam the streets and parks, often in packs.

There are at least 500,000 of them out there right now.

Left to themselves, the figure would be close to 4 million in ten years' time.

Homeless dogs cause road accidents, attack livestock and foul our parks and pavements.

And yet we can't blame the dogs, for we live in a society that makes it more difficult to own a television than a living, breathing creature.

There is no licence required. The Government abolished the licence last year and we are now seeing the consequences.

The RSPCA want to see a dog registration scheme introduced.

And so it seems do most of you. In a recent poll, 92% of you said "yes" to registration.

If there was a registration fee it would encourage responsible dog-ownership.

Each dog could be identified with a number so that its owner

could be traced and held responsible for the dog's actions.

The money raised would finance a national dog warden scheme, more efficient clean-up operations and more education for dog-owners.

These measures seem so sensible you wonder why they haven't been tried before.

Well, many of them have.

Sweden, America, Germany, Australia, Russia, France and Ireland all have a more enlightened policy than Britain.

Help us catch up.

Write to your MP and press for dog registration.

If you're not sure how to go about it, call free on 0800 400478 and we'll give you an action-pack and add your name to our petition.

Do it now, for every day that goes by sees another 1,000 dogs put down.

And what kind of society kills healthy dogs?

Registration, not extermination.

WITHOUT SUCH A SIMPLE PRECAUTION
THE JEOPARDY OF LIFE IS IMMENSELY INCREASED.

It is a convention of advertising to make claims for products which are hard to prove, as in this advert.

upheld and the advert was withdrawn.

The RSPCA obviously has an interest in asserting the link: the organization wishes to draw attention to the increased number of unwanted dogs. But what was the interest of the two MPs and member of the public quoted in *The Guardian* in September 1989 'who questioned whether the problem of stray dogs had grown worse since licences were scrapped'? Were they members of the government which had done away with the licence, perhaps? Or were they other people also embarrassed by the advert or with an interest in stopping it? Questions like these are important to ask so that we can work out our own positions.

Some complaints are made by individuals on behalf of groups in society who are offended by certain adverts. Many of these complaints concern nudity or aspects of sexual behaviour which shock some people, leading them to seek bans on particular adverts which they consider 'indecent'.

Other complaints, however, seek changes to advertising in general. Women might complain about adverts they find sexist, or members of minority ethnic groups might complain about adverts they find racist. Few of these complaints are upheld because they are not covered by the Code. The offence is not caused by a demonstrable dishonesty or untruthfulness. Nor may the adverts be considered indecent.

Advertising control
In China and the USSR, advertising is controlled by the government via agencies set up by and accountable to the state. Where agencies are more independent of government control, they are normally only accountable to themselves. Furthermore, many of these authorities are staffed by experts connected with the advertising industry itself.

Charities have learned the value of advertising to raise funds. The Multiple Sclerosis Society has concentrated on the shocking and debilitating aspects of this illness in order to bring the message home.

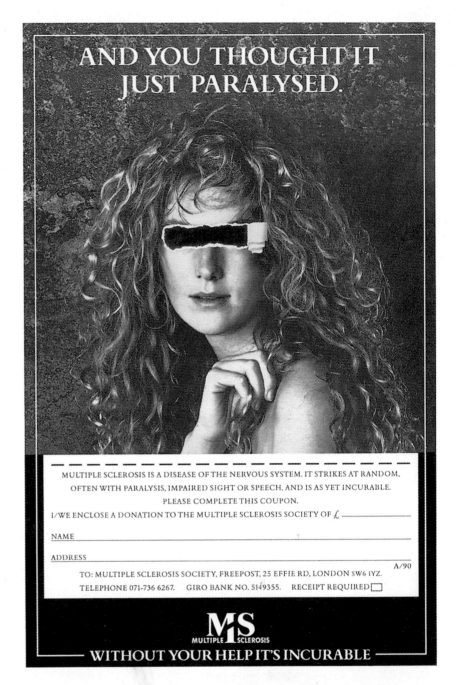

AND YOU THOUGHT IT JUST PARALYSED.

MULTIPLE SCLEROSIS IS A DISEASE OF THE NERVOUS SYSTEM. IT STRIKES AT RANDOM, OFTEN WITH PARALYSIS, IMPAIRED SIGHT OR SPEECH, AND IS AS YET INCURABLE. PLEASE COMPLETE THIS COUPON.
I/WE ENCLOSE A DONATION TO THE MULTIPLE SCLEROSIS SOCIETY OF £ _____

NAME _____

ADDRESS _____
                                                                          A/90
TO: MULTIPLE SCLEROSIS SOCIETY, FREEPOST, 25 EFFIE RD, LONDON SW6 1YZ.
TELEPHONE 071-736 6267.   GIRO BANK NO. 5149355.   RECEIPT REQUIRED ☐

MULTIPLE SCLEROSIS

WITHOUT YOUR HELP IT'S INCURABLE

1   Are you aware of any adverts that do not seem to conform to the Code of Advertising: how did they breach the Code?
2   Do you think the RSPCA advert breached the Code: why was it withdrawn?
3   Do you think adverts that offend some women and ethnic minorities breach the spirit, if not the letter, of the Code?
4   How would you amend the Code to stop adverts causing this kind of offence?

For critics who support complaints such as these, the Code seems biased. That is, it favours those groups such as the MPs in the RSPCA case, who are powerful enough to put pressure on the regulating authority. Other critics see the Code as incomplete and therefore not powerful enough to help many among the ordinary people it was set up to protect (as in the case of the women or ethnic minorities).

2 Attitudes to advertising

There are three common and pervasive general attitudes to advertising. There are those that support advertising; those seeking more controls and changes; and finally, those that fundamentally disagree with the whole principle of advertising. This chapter looks at some of the arguments that arise from all three attitudes.

Among supporters, advertisers are their own best advocates, as we might expect:

> Advertising . . . can be used personally, for example, in classified advertising, as well as publicly, but its main economic interest is as part of the marketing process . . . The business of advertising is therefore the business of commerce. It works to help achieve commercial objectives. Since advertising is discretionary [a matter of choice], and advertising funds might otherwise go to corporate profits, it has to achieve these objectives to justify itself. Companies do not spend hard-earned money on advertising unless they have to, and if they spend it, it must work. (David Farbey, *The Business of Advertising*, 1979.)

This advert for the New Zealand butter company, Anchor, caught the audience's attention by the amusing spectacle of dairy cows playing football.

David Farbey supports advertising because it works for advertisers. Torin Douglas, on the other hand, finds that advertising works for consumers:

> The people who make adverts are dealing in people's dreams, hopes and fears, touching aspirations, providing reassurance and making as their contribution to this mad mosaic that is life an offering of just about the only good news that is fit to print. Advertising [is] the most efficient means of letting the maker of the product or provider of the service inform enough prospective users of what is available. (Torin Douglas, *The Complete Guide to Advertising*, 1984.)

1   According to members of the advertising industry, such as David Farbey and Torin Douglas, what is it about advertising that 'works'?
2   Do you think it works equally as well for the consumer as the advertiser?

Right *This poster appeals to people's desire to escape from their surroundings for a while into a world of dream and promise.*

Below *British Rail makes fun of aging pop star Gary Glitter in this Saatchi & Saatchi advert for a Young Person's Railcard.*

Save money with a Young Persons Railcard.
(Keep trying Gary).

Young Persons Railcard.

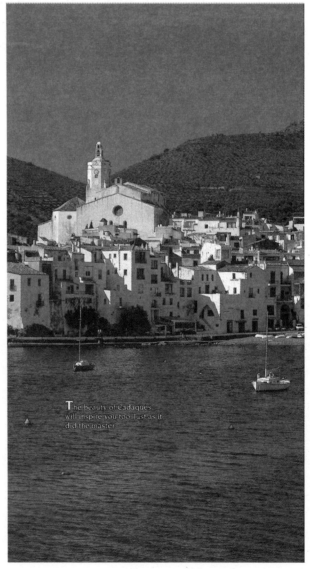

The beauty of Cadaqués will inspire you too. Just as it did the master.

An enchanting place to Dali.

Dali found the village of Cadaqués so enchanting he chose to make his home there.

You too will find it an exquisite place to dally.

And like him you will be spoiled for choice.

To the north on the Atlantic side, to the south along the Mediterranean coast, and in the Balearic Islands, you will find equally enchanting white-washed, sun-lit fishing villages. Each has its own personality and charm – catering for every mood.

In just a few metres the bustle of street cafes is contrasted by the solitude of peaceful coves. In every fishing village you will find the amazing seafood restaurants for which Spain is famous.

Like Dali, you won't want to tear yourself away.

Spain. Everything under the sun.

ESPAÑA

For further information please contact
The Spanish Tourist Office, 57 St. James's Street,
London SW1A 1LD. Tel: 071-499 4593.
Telex: 888138. Prestel: 34429.

Point of sale advertising directs the customer's attention to the products on sale.

At the beginning of this century great claims were made by some that advertising would bring wealth to all nations. Others remain more cynical of the motives of those making such claims. Read here what two critics have to say:

> With the wide-scale implementation of mass production in the 1920s, advertising and the ideal of mass consumption were catapulted to the foreground of modern economic planning . . . American businessmen celebrated the coming of the new industrial age as one which would accelerate social progress among the masses and at the same time vindicate [justify] 'the great stream of human selfishness' of which they were an undeniable part. (Stuart Ewen, *Captains of Consciousness: Advertising and the Social Roots of the Consumer Culture*, 1976.)

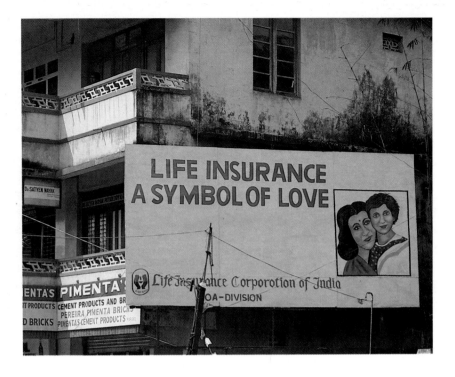

A common advertising ploy is to connect the most mundane product with an attractive lifestyle, high social status or, as here, motherly love.

| What attitudes to consumers do commentators such as Stuart Ewen and E S Turner discern among advertisers?
2 What do you see as the prime object of advertising?

> No one doubts that advertising has done much to raise the standards of physical well-being. The catalogue of its benefits is a long one . . . It has brought prosperity to communities . . . By widening markets, it has enabled costs of raw materials to be cut, accelerated turnover, lowered selling prices. It has . . . kept people in employment. It has given a guarantee of dependability — for who would buy a nameless car put together in a back-street shop? These gratifying results have been achieved, not only by information, but by persuasive and indeed intimidating advertisements. The prime object was not, of course, to benefit humanity but to sell more fabrics, more toothpaste, more disinfectant. (E S Turner, *The Shocking History of Advertising*, 1952.)

Both of these commentators recognize the benefits advertising brings but are more suspicious of the motives of advertisers. The first commentator goes so far as to say that advertising appeals to the selfishness of humans, that as they are naturally greedy, little encouragement is needed for people to want to buy yet more and more goods.

There are other critics still who dislike advertising not so much for the intentions of the advertisers but for the effects they propose it has on us as consumers:

> *Do you find yourself being persuaded by adverts into buying things you do not really need?*
> *2 Do you think others are affected in this way?*
> *3 Does it matter?*

> One of the major criticisms of advertising is that it makes us too materialistic by persuading us, for instance, that we can achieve certain desirable goals in life through possessing things in a cycle of continuous and conspicuous consumption. (Gillian Dyer, *Advertising as Communication*, 1982.)

An extension of this argument is that not only can advertising persuade us to buy things we do not really need or even want, but that it works to create in us those needs and wants. Worse, the fear is that advertising may tap into our baser motives, what Stuart Ewen called above 'the great stream of human selfishness'. A supporter of the advertising industry describes an argument often used to attack it:

> Advertising creates false and materialistic demands for things people do not really need or want. Indeed, it may well be asked do people need false eyelashes or wigs; was it necessary for detergents to be introduced in competition with soap flakes; wouldn't it be better if there were fewer cars; don't all these cars mean that our towns are cluttered up with petrol pumps; are we so weak and lazy we can no longer peel potatoes; and must we eat so many sweets, drink so much beer, smoke so many cigars, feed so many cats and dogs . . .? (Frank Jefkins, *Advertising*, 1982.)

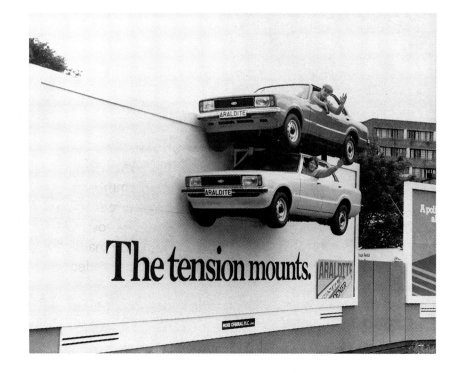

All sorts of gimmicks are used in adverts. Following on from a campaign where a car was stuck with Araldite to a billboard, this poster shows two Ford Cortina cars over the catchy copyline 'The tension mounts.'

Finally, some critics fear that advertising sells more than the goods it brings to our attention. Gillian Dyer argues the case that, although people . . .

> . . . might not believe the claims made for a product by an advertiser (such as 'Persil washes whiter'), they might find it more difficult to resist the more general social image or message presented along with the overt sales pitch — for example, that we can make friends by drinking the right kind of beer, get a boyfriend by using the right kind of shampoo, become a supermum to an adoring family by buying the right tin of baked beans, or avoid being a social outcast and guilt feelings if we buy life assurance. (Gillian Dyer, *Advertising as Communication*, 1982.)

According to this argument, advertising sells dreams that are false or unobtainable. It lies to us or fools us. Even worse, it encourages undesirable qualities in human nature:

> Since [television adverts] sell goods by holding up certain attitudes as admirable, it seems obvious that they are at the same time and to some degree 'selling' the attitudes also . . . the attitudes and values which act as vehicles for the sale of the goods are themselves being 'sold'. (*Report of the Pilkington Committee on Broadcasting*, 1960.)

American adverts are allowed to mention and even criticize their competitors.

This advertisement is clearly aimed at young people: the lifestyle is presented as being as attractive as the Converse All Stars boots.

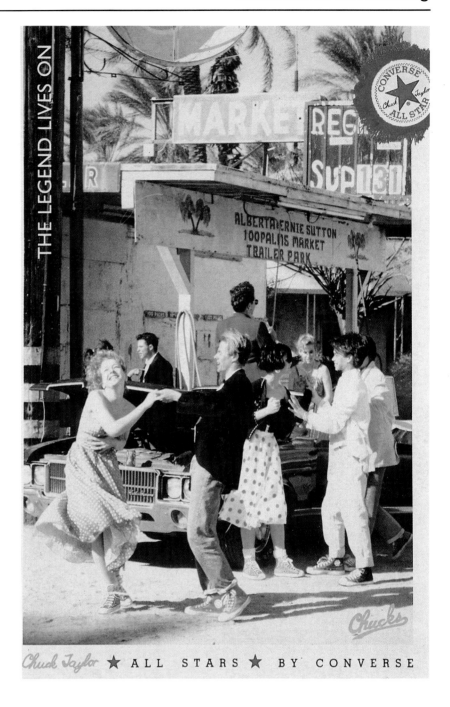

THE LEGEND LIVES ON

Chuck Taylor ★ ALL STARS ★ BY CONVERSE

Who pays for advertising?
The costs of advertising are met by the consumer: about 15 per cent of a purchase price is attributed directly to advertising costs.

These attitudes might be to do with the way we are supposed to live, the jobs we are supposed to have and the clothes we are supposed to wear. The argument here is that people are influenced by the whole 'package' the advertisement offers: it is not enough to merely enjoy Coca-Cola, for example, but we must also be young, fashionable and have lots of friends.

Advertising photographers command large fees for skills in lighting and composing photographs.

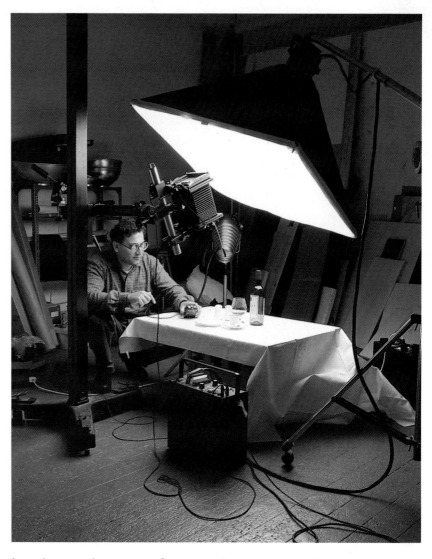

> In countless ways often unnoticed we are led to accept as common ground a world in which the key to happiness is the possession of the newest model of car, dining-room suite, refrigerator and television set, in which any malaise can be neutralized . . . and in which the chosen reward for a hard day's work is to 'treat yourself' to a luxury you can't afford because you feel you 'deserve it' or even 'owe it to yourself'. (Frank Whitehead, *Advertising*, in Denys Thompson (editor), *Discrimination and Popular Culture*, 1964.)

These arguments that advertising works on us in hidden and unconscious ways are more complex than the arguments we met earlier. The next chapter looks at some of these arguments more closely.

1 Have you ever been made to feel worried or anxious about your appearance or behaviour by the way in which an advert sold a product? If so, how and why?
2 Do you think advertising can sell attitudes as well as goods?
3 Do you agree that these attitudes are undesirable?

Advertising as control

> How long would it take, without television advertising, for people to discover the numerous soft drinks that exist or the variety of babies' nappies? What is more, because of the speed with which you can bring products to the market you can correspondingly quickly move on to the next technology. The learning curve of the manufacturer is thus speeded up and, in order to get an edge, he keeps on trying to develop a better product. (Brian Henry (editor), *British Television Advertising: The First 30 Years*, 1986.)

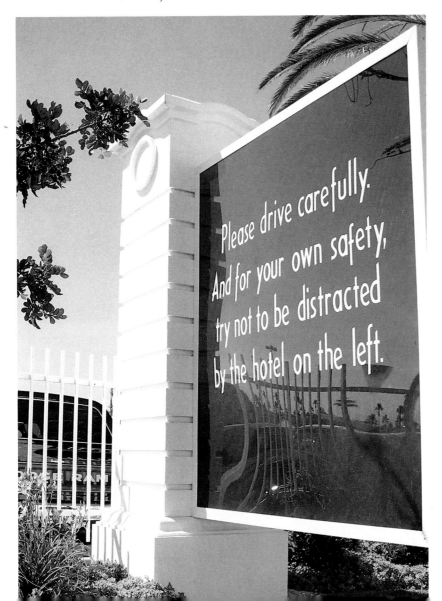

Adverts can control or direct our responses in very clever ways: by asking us not to look at the hotel on the left, this notice instantly arouses our curiosity.

Advertising surrounds us. Whether in the local high street, on the tube or train, or on a major road such as this one in Japan, billboards and posters often dominate the scene.

What Brian Henry here calls 'the learning curve' makes the treatment of us as consumers sound more friendly than threatening. After all, where is the harm in advertisers using television, or any effective means possible, to bring new products speedily to our attention?

Vance Packard has one answer. He worries about this practice in advertising:

> Large scale efforts are being made, often with impressive success, to channel our unthinking habits, our purchasing decisions, and our thought processes by the use of insights gleaned from psychiatry and the social sciences . . . The use of mass psychoanalysis to guide campaigns of persuasion has become the basis of a multi-million dollar industry. (Vance Packard, *The Hidden Persuaders*, 1957, quoted in Kathy Myers, *Understains*, 1986.)

Packard's worry is that people are being virtually hypnotized into buying advertised products, unconsciously manipulated by advertising in order for companies to gain vast profits.

To some critics, advertising is even more dangerous than this. It is a part and parcel of an economic system which takes advantage of working people. Author Stuart Ewen argues that the advertising industry tries to sell us not just goods, nor just attitudes, but a whole way of life. And the way of life being sold is one we are all familiar with in western countries and their capitalist economies. Critics of advertising are often also critics of capitalism. They argue that both advertising and capitalism emphasise greed, self-interest and mindless consumption.

Other critics, however, disagree that this is the inevitable nature of advertising. They are concerned not so much about advertising itself but about the way it is organized. Some groups of people in society have much more money and power to advertise than others. Most of us, therefore, are in an unequal relationship with the advertising industry: we are always consumers, never producers of advertising.

The Saatchi brothers set up their now internationally famous agency at the end of the 1960s.

Minority interest programmes

Tim Brady, head of corporate sponsorship at Thames, the richest ITV company, said the programme *The Concert* needed its £50,000 sponsorship from McEwen's lager. 'Audiences at 1.15am are tiny and programmes at that time attract very little advertising revenue. Without sponsorship, the series simply would not have been made.'

The corporate image of Shell was celebrated in the 1930s through these commissioned pieces of art. The bottom row of pictures shows some more conventional black and white adverts for Shell.

A further development of this argument is that wealthy and powerful organizations are able to keep themselves in the public eye and popularize their own opinions. In this way they do not advertise their products but themselves.

> Towards the end of the 1970s corporate advertising came along in a big way. Although ICI were the first to run a corporate campaign, with 'The Pathfinders' and 'Ideas in Action', the one with the most impact was Dunlop, which Saatchi's [an advertising agency] did. It showed a girl playing tennis with all the things Dunlop made disappearing, to the line 'Imagine how much you would miss Dunlop'. (Brian Henry (editor), *British Television Advertising: The First 30 Years,* 1986.)

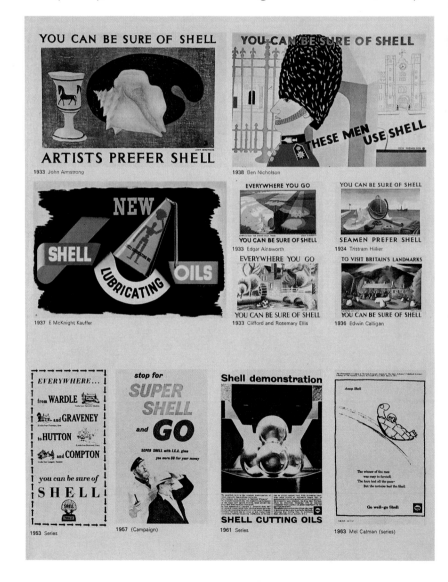

Fashion designers such as Yves Saint Laurent promote their work through clothes shows, as well as by advertisements in magazines and on billboards.

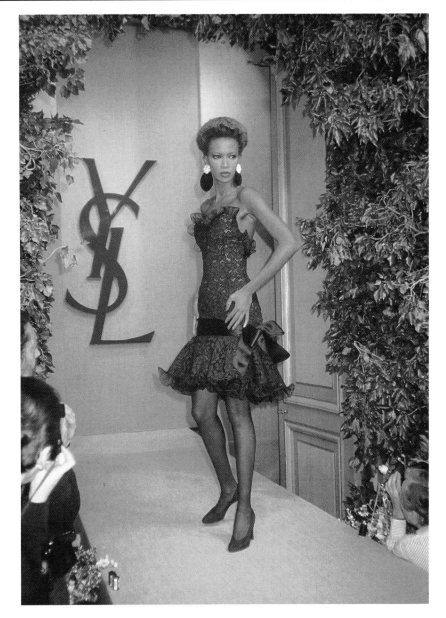

Sponsorship

Can sponsored programmes be free from bias? In 1959, the producers of a US television drama about the Nuremberg war crimes trials were made to drop the words 'gas chamber' from the film's soundtrack: the sponsor was the American Gas Association.

In a 1989 UK survey of 150 top advertisers, 50 per cent of marketing directors said they believed that sponsors should influence programme content.

Organizations have been promoting their names for many years, however, through sponsoring such things as sports events, theatre and, in some countries, television programmes.

Advertising by sponsorship is an increasing practice. Events may be specially staged to attract the attention of journalists and broadcasters. Tobacco firms sponsor sporting events so that the names of their products and companies will be displayed on football jerseys or racing cars. Chocolate bar companies give grants to touring arts groups and exhibitions so that their names will be mentioned and caught by the cameras.

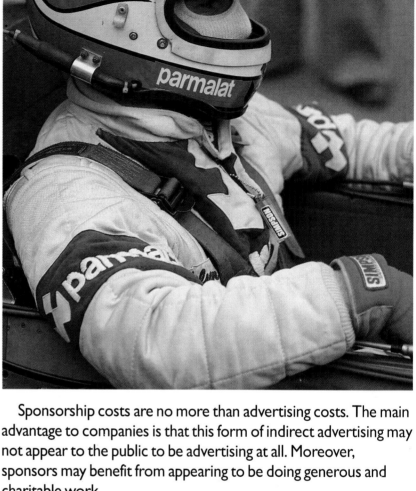

This racing driver is sponsored by Parmalat. He is paid to display the name Parmalat on his clothing.

Sponsorship costs are no more than advertising costs. The main advantage to companies is that this form of indirect advertising may not appear to the public to be advertising at all. Moreover, sponsors may benefit from appearing to be doing generous and charitable work.

More recently, however, advertisers have found even more indirect ways of advertising:

> Many companies and advertising agencies now spend a great deal of time producing, not advertisements, but advertorials, i.e. thinly disguised advertising copy, much of which finds its way into the media in the form of news stories. Since these stories keep the manufacturer's name in the public eye without incurring advertising costs, many companies now spend much time and ingenuity in planning them. (Len Masterman, *Teaching the Media*, 1985.)

Political broadcasts

In Britain, the broadcasting authorities take the view that a political broadcast should last for at least five minutes. In the USA, political commercials can last for as short a length of time as 30 seconds. An advantage of the shorter length of time is that political broadcasts can be more flexible.

24

The danger of advertorials is that what is in fact an advertisement is 'disguised' as a news story or unbiased fact. The public is, then, likely to be less cautious in its judgement on the product: most people will not believe everything that something which is obviously an advertisement says.

The same kind of practice has been taken over by modern politicians such as George Bush, Margaret Thatcher and Bob Hawke. All have run political campaigns and party political television broadcasts which employ many of the devices, and sometimes even the agencies, of the advertising industry.

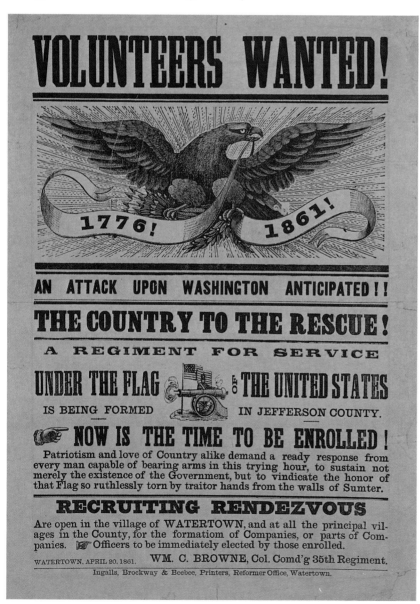

An 1861 American recruitment poster belonging to the near-vanished age of information-based advertisements. Today, the design or image of an advertisement is as important as the factual content.

1   What is the difference between advertising and propaganda?
2   When the British government advertises the sale of public utilities such as national telephone systems and gas companies as part of its plan to privatize the public sector, is that advertising or propaganda?
3   When a company provides an advertorial or stage manages a news event to promote its name, is that free advertising or free propaganda?
4   Has the advertising industry become part of corporate and government attempts to control both markets and public opinion?

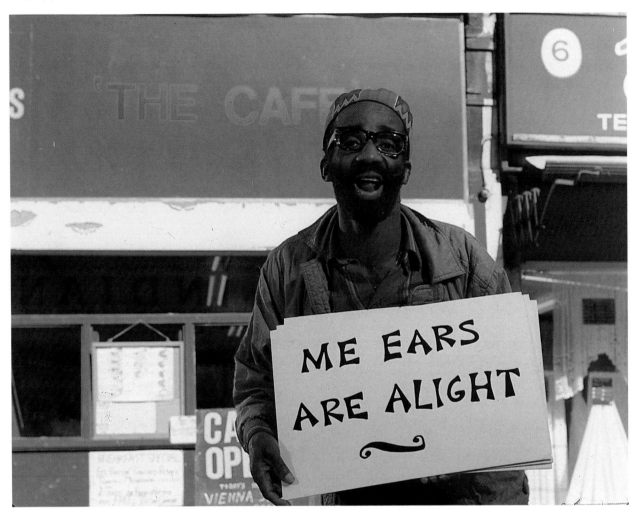

Many critics are worried that these developments turn political campaigns into advertising, with politicians being sold like brand names. Modern corporations, and even public institutions such as governments, make use of the advertising industry to sell their policies as well as their products. Many critics worry about this trend in advertising everything and anything. In particular, they worry that people may be persuaded not by corporate or political policies, but by the best advertising campaign. In the past, politicians relied more on their own skills in giving out information about themselves or their parties. The way in which this was done was often very crude. The trend with advertising, however, is to present the message in as slick a way as possible. Critics of this development are concerned that these powerful groups and organizations use advertising in hidden ways to control public opinion in their own interests.

Above *This Maxell Tapes advert taps into the popularity and appeal of youth cultures. Because an inferior quality tape is being played, the man in the advert mishears the words of a popular Desmond Dekker song and the chorus 'The Israelites' becomes 'Me Ears Are Alight'.*

Right *Political parties increasingly employ advertisers to promote their policies, just as manufacturers employ advertisers to promote their goods.*

800,000 PEOPLE ARE WAITING TO GO INTO HOSPITAL. THEY'RE BEING HELD UP BY THE PRIME MINISTER'S HEART PROBLEM.

The Conservative Party's cold-hearted policies are crippling the National Health Service.

221 hospitals have been shut down since they came to power, and spending on the rest has been cut by millions.

If this Government doesn't give a damn about the thousands of people waiting for operations, then the country urgently needs one that does.

THE COUNTRY'S CRYING OUT FOR LABOUR.

4

Who does advertising think you are?
– The case of women

All advertisers must have a clear idea of who they are advertising their products to. They therefore do a great deal of market research to check that they are speaking to the consumers they have in mind. One problem some critics see arising from this is that advertisers regularly tend to depict in their adverts the same types of people they see as their ideal consumer.

> Most housewives have to think up several meals a day and are delighted by new meal ideas. If it's something that gives them the chance to get a new nod, a different reaction, from the family, then they'll be very pleased with it. (Warren Goodwin, quoted by Ian Walker, *'Thirty Second Dream Pushers',* Leveller magazine, December 1977.)

The speaker here, Warren Goodwin, works for an advertising agency. The ideal consumer he talks about is a busy housewife with a large family, always eager for new food products to try out. It is no surprise to find such a figure selling domestic products in adverts, for example the mother in the British OXO adverts.

Some critics of advertising are concerned about how this interest commonly results in adverts using stereotypes of people:

> Even the most cursory research quickly revealed many 'humorous' advertisements populated by nagging wives, unceasingly talkative girlfriends, dreadful women drivers, hopelessly dumb blondes. Women are often made absurdly ecstatic by very simple products, as though a brand new floor cleaner or deodorant really could make all the difference of a lifetime. One 1978 investigation of 39 television commercials found they showed two country ladies, one woman as party adornment – and eighteen housewives preparing food, washing up, ironing, cleaning and sitting with their families. These women were shown as completely fulfilled by a caring, nurturing domestic role, but also continually in need of advice from various 'expert' males about how to run their homes. (Jane Root, *Pictures of Women,* 1984.)

Feminist critics of advertising such as Jane Root see in this tendency the constant narrowing down of possible roles for women. They argue that if women are always being 'addressed' as mothers and housewives, they will come to think this is the only right way to be. Following on from such portrayals others will judge women by the extent to which they perform in these roles.

Another argument commonly made by critics concerns the other major stereotype of women – as the glamorous consumers of toiletries and as appealing decoration for cars or other products for men.

These actresses were called the kiss or kill girls as part of the promotion for a Hollywood film in the 1960s. This type of stereotype which suggests that women are simply sex symbols persists even today.

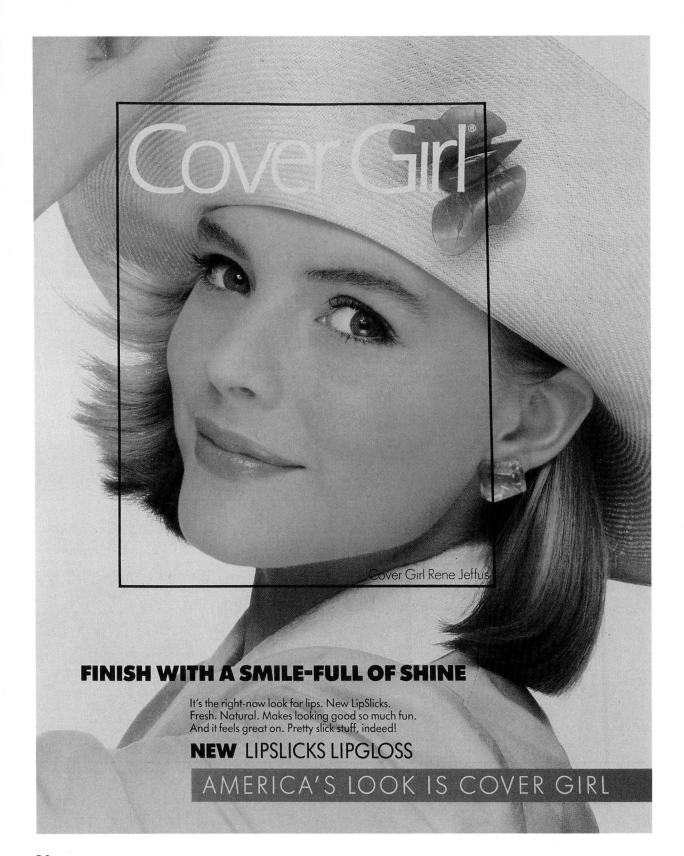

Cover Girl Rene Jeffus

FINISH WITH A SMILE-FULL OF SHINE

It's the right-now look for lips. New LipSlicks.
Fresh. Natural. Makes looking good so much fun.
And it feels great on. Pretty slick stuff, indeed!

NEW LIPSLICKS LIPGLOSS

AMERICA'S LOOK IS COVER GIRL

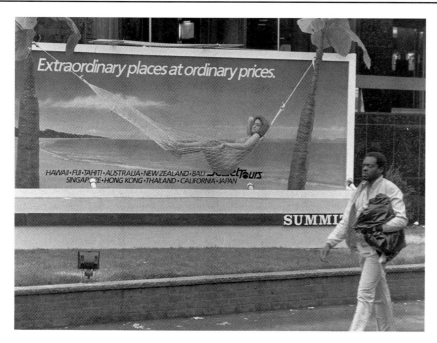

Extraordinary places at ordinary prices.

HAWAII · FIJI · TAHITI · AUSTRALIA · NEW ZEALAND · BALI · Jetset Tours
SINGAPORE · HONG KONG · THAILAND · CALIFORNIA · JAPAN

SUMMI

Left *Model Tina Hudson poses live for Jetset Tours. The man walking along the street, however, is oblivious to both the model and the advertisement. How much do sexist adverts really influence our perceptions and behaviour?*

> The majority of women who appear in advertisements are distinguished by their youth and beauty. They are the 'girlfriends' who appear alongside their men in shampoo and chocolate advertisements, and the sensuous 'models' who act as status-giving accessories to successful men. Other similarly sexual women, often clothed in very little, can be seen languorously sprawled over car bonnets or enticingly wrapped around stereos . . . Many women who thought about these images discovered that they felt insulted, demeaned and embarrassed by them. (Jane Root, *Pictures of Women*, 1984.)

It is not just that women may be upset by these images, however. It has been argued that such images have an effect on men's attitudes to women. Men come to think of women only as sexual objects, as bodies or even bits of bodies, over which they have the right to assume control.

> Of course, it is not the case that [the man] is being told that he instantly would be able to attract this kind of woman if he buys a particular camera or car. But . . . the potential buyer is being asked to bask in the agreeable sensation of power and control which images of near-naked women suggest to men in this society. In order for this to happen — and for the advertisement to make sense to him — he must think of the woman in the advertisement as a thing over which he has control. (Jane Root, *Pictures of Women*, 1984.)

Opposite page *Advertisers encourage women to make themselves look as attractive as possible.*

And what of adverts featuring women like this aimed not at men but at women?

> One of the pleasures which the advertising industry offers women is the promise of a kind of power and self-determination. Images of women marketed to women rarely present female sexuality purely in terms of vulnerability, accessibility or availability. But the power which the advertising of beauty and personal products offers women is always of a limited kind, located in terms of sexual display, appearance and attractiveness. (Kathy Myers, *Understains*, 1986.)

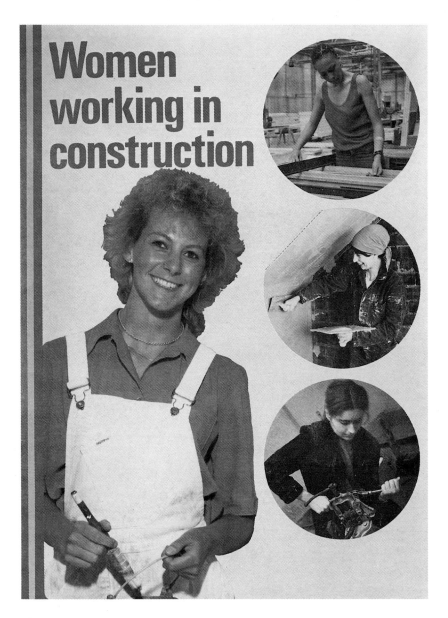

Women working in construction

This advertisement is trying to draw women in to the construction industry by showing women in roles which are conventionally regarded as male.

1   Much of the debate about stereotyping in advertising has taken place among feminist critics worried about the effects of certain images of women in advertising. The same kinds of arguments could be made about other social types, too. What does it mean for relationships between men and women when men are always represented as tough and powerful figures?
2   What does it mean for relationships between various age groups when children and old people are too often represented as dependent, at risk and in need of protection?

How do people respond to advertising?

For the critics we have met so far, advertising has been judged by the effects it has on us as people in our everyday lives. For the advertising industry, the most important effect is on how we act as consumers. Advertisers want us to buy the products they advertise, so they judge the power of an advert by the success it has in persuading us to buy the product advertised.

Some critics complain that adverts have the effect of turning us into manic consumers, buying against our will. They maintain that adverts make us conservative thinkers, passively accepting what adverts lead us to believe is 'the good life'.

All these arguments about the effects of advertising assume we have very little control over what happens to us when we come into contact with advertising. They all take for granted the idea that since advertising sees us only as consumers, that is indeed all we are.

The neon lights of the advertisements at Causeway Bay, Hong Kong, make for a brilliant night-time spectacle.

The Pepsi campaign uses famous names such as Tina Turner and David Bowie to sell the product.

But it is not as simple as that. We can think of ways in which we use advertising that are unimportant to advertisers but very important to us. Critics who hold this view make different arguments about how we use advertising, but all agree that we are not just passive consumers but active users of advertising.

For two artists in the USA, one particular form of advertising especially brings colour, vitality and spectacle into our lives:

Audience appeal

Many Hollywood stars appear in Japanese advertisements. Eddie Murphy was paid $3 million for advertising Toyota's latest saloon car. What is right for the Japanese audience, however, is not necessarily big business elsewhere: actors insist on special clauses in their contracts which guarantee that the adverts will never be shown in the USA or Europe.

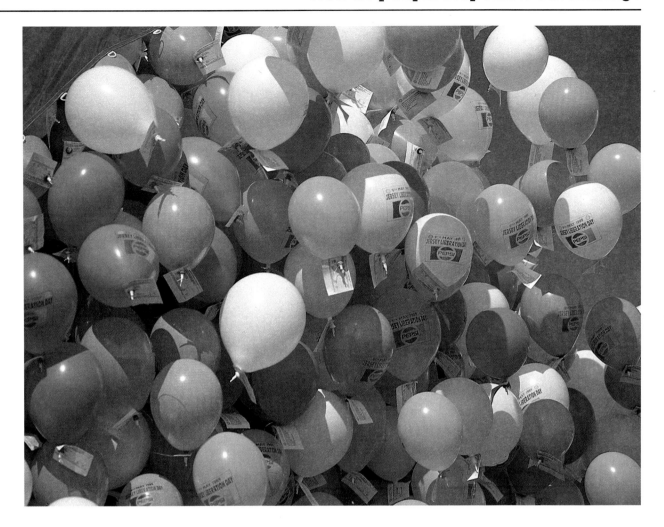

> . . . consider the glamorous character billboards add to certain areas of the world. London's Piccadilly Circus, New York's Times Square, Tokyo's Ginza, the Strip in Las Vegas and Sunset Boulevard in Los Angeles — all these places have a special attraction, an enchantment. The excitement generated by these billboards and neon media art forms have made each area uniquely famous. (Sally Henderson and Robert Landau, *Billboard Art*, 1981.)

These coloured balloons which were released in Jersey formed another type of promotion for Pepsi.

These critics are not interested in the purpose of the adverts. What they register is the beauty they see such adverts collectively bringing to certain urban environments. Not all billboard advertising is this spectacular, however. Nor do all critics agree about its artistry. Some critics find advertising an intrusion into social spaces such as streets, especially where the advertisers' messages give offence.

In common with many other capital squares, Times Square, New York, presents a vast array of advertisements.

> [An] ad was opposite my place of work. I had to stare at it out of the window. A colleague and I went out and added the graffiti. You can see there are two handwritings! It was a way of taking over the poster. You have to have a lot of money to afford billboards like that. We wanted to reclaim the open spaces that have been colonised by advertisers. By writing angry but humorous graffiti, we were also making the point that ad agencies don't have the monopoly on wit. It feels great to see it reproduced everywhere. It's made the point that women can do something instead of just seethe.
> (Quoted in Jill Posner, *Spray it Loud*, 1982.)

Spray-painters treat billboards as canvasses, literally commenting on posters. They talk back to advertisers and talk to passers-by about the attitudes they see the adverts expressing. They do so directly, treating billboards as a communal space in which to express their views. As such, their concern is to resist their roles as consumers. Instead, they become social commentators, actively using advertising but for purposes never dreamed of by the advertisers.

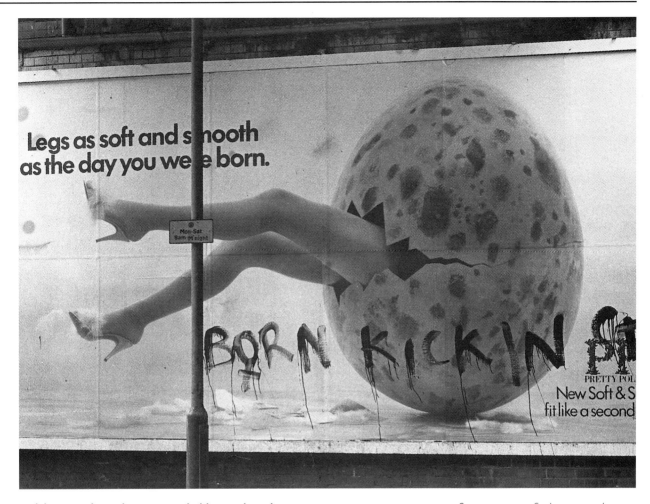

Legs as soft and smooth
as the day you were born.

Mon-Sat
8am-Midnight

BORN KICKIN

PRETTY POL
New Soft & S
fit like a second

No wonder advertisers dislike and seek to prosecute spray-painters. Of course, spray-painting, like all forms of graffiti, is an illegal act. In Australia, a group called Billboard Utilising Graffitists Against Unhealthy Promotions (BUGA UP) has been defacing tobacco adverts since 1979. Some of its members have been arrested and even imprisoned:

> We would prefer to go to jail rather than pay the fines imposed if we're caught. That's one form of protest, following on from the protest we make on the billboard. I was accused of 'malicious damage' to a billboard. I don't even swat flies. That's how malicious I am. (Quoted in Jill Posner, *Spray it Loud*, 1982.)

Another critic has drawn attention to some bizarre results that occur when adverts are seen in unexpected environments or combinations. (The following quotation has been adapted from a description of an advert and a news photograph in a newspaper colour supplement.)

Some women feel so strongly about sexism in advertising that they paint graffiti on billboard posters to explain their opposition and change the meaning of the advert.

A double-page spread in a magazine unintentionally reveals the contrast between the manufactured world of advertising and the devastating effects of the earthquake dealt with in the facing article.

> The contrast between publicity's interpretation of the world and the world's actual condition is a very stark one, and this sometimes becomes evident . . . The shock of such contrasts is considerable: not only because of the coexistence of the two worlds shown, but also because of the cynicism of the culture which shows them . . . It can be argued that the juxtaposition of images was not planned. Nevertheless the text, the photographs taken . . . , the layout of the publicity, the printing of both, the fact that (they) cannot be co-ordinated — all these are produced by the same culture. (John Berger, *Ways of Seeing*, 1976.)

The writer draws our attention to the shock we experience when we see wealth and poverty side by side. For John Berger, the contrast between the glamorous world of the advert and the harsh reality of life around it condemns the advertisers and the society that tolerates such an imbalance.

What we actually do with such experiences, however, is

debatable. Some would say that we begin to passively accept them or put them from our minds in order not to be overwhelmed by them. Others would say we learn from such experiences and feel moved to put right the conditions that produce our shocked reaction. In this way, the situations in which we regularly meet advertising can be at least as important to us as advertising itself.

It might be, indeed, that how advertising enters into our daily lives is more important to us than how it enters into our purses. If so, it may be that rather than making us less sensitive to the world about us, we can learn from occurences like this and become more understanding.

Regardless, then, of how advertisers hope that we will react, our actual responses may be very much more varied. Rather than using advertising simply as consumers, we can use it as art, as social comment or as education. Thinking like this means that we can see ourselves as participants in (as well as observers of) the world in which advertising is just one part.

1 How aware are you of advertising? Are you aware of different forms of it on the streets, on television or in newspapers and magazines?
2 Do you use advertising for different purposes at different times?
3 What would you do if you saw an advert that shocked or offended you?

This photograph taken in Bombay contrasts the colourful world of advertising and the depressing context of poverty in which it is sometimes seen.

6

Children and advertising

All regulating authorities have special codes for advertising for children. The ASA has five main guidelines, each one typical of those relating to children in nations all over the world:

● Adverts should not exploit children's lack of experience or willingness to believe.

● Adverts should cause no physical, mental or moral harm to children.

● Adverts should not make children feel inferior because they do not own the product advertised.

● Adverts should not encourage children to pester others to buy products advertised.

● Adverts in which children appear should not show the children in dangerous situations, nor should the adverts encourage unsafe behaviour in children.

Most of these guidelines seem reasonable, although when applied some may prove more difficult to judge than others. Given that most children have no money of their own to spend, could any advert avoid 'encouraging children to pester others to buy' the product advertised if they wanted it? It would be hard to distinguish the difference between the success of an advert selling a product

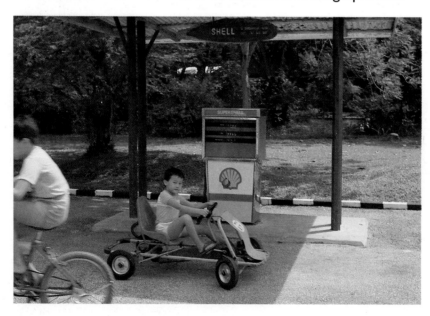

The marketing of products now invades every area of our lives. Here, the Shell symbol in this children's playground is taken for granted by the children playing in front of it.

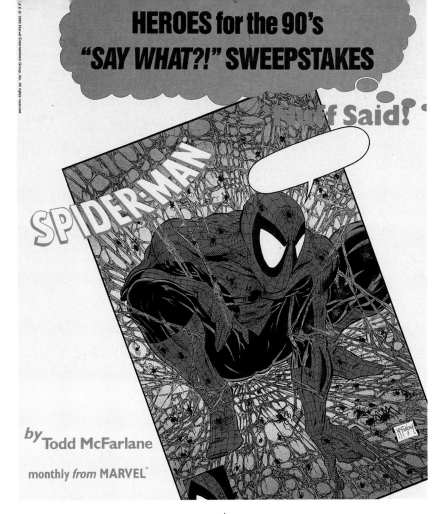

Marvel comics promote Spiderman by encouraging children to enter their 'Sweepstakes' competition.

and the child's desire for that product, regardless of how attractive the advert has made it seem.

Some critics find the whole idea of advertising to children especially undesirable, fearing that its power can influence children's minds:

> We tried an experiment the other evening . . . To a curly-headed four-year-old being tucked under the covers we posed this question: 'Susie, which product brushes teeth whiter?' 'Colgate's of course, Gramp.' We couldn't resist another. 'Which product washes clothes cleaner?' Without a moment's hesitation: 'Tide . . .' Where else on earth is brand consciousness firmly fixed in the minds of four-year-old tots? How many pre-school age Americans are pre-sold on how many different products? How can we get reliable data? What is it worth to a manufacturer who can close in on this juvenile audience and continue to sell under controlled conditions . . .? (Quoted by E S Turner, *The Shocking History of Advertising*, 1952.)

The marketing strategy for Teenage Mutant Hero Turtles has proved as effective as that adopted by the producers of Care Bears, Thundercats and My Little Pony.

Another critic sees this as more of a parental worry, that other groups outside the home are competing with their authority:

> Throughout the community there is a stir and excitement that is reflecting on the children. There are so many desirable luxuries in the world now, so many revealed by advertising . . . All these things make the lot of the housewife harder in so far as the training of her children is concerned. She is dealing with a more alert, more sophisticated, more sensuous child — and one who knows his place and power. (Abraham Myerson, *The Nervous Housewife*, 1929.)

Perhaps it is easier to take sides in this debate when we are sure of the child's knowledge as to what is and what is not an advert. What about those cases where the line between advertising and child entertainment is fudged, however?

In the USA in recent times, cinema films and television programmes have been made with characters that are then sold as toys. The film *Star Wars* was massively popular and made over $400 million in 1984. But this is only a part of the vast profits made from merchandising *Star Wars* figures and machines as toys. Television cartoon series featuring characters sold as soft toys are now regularly offered at no cost to television channels. Each time they are screened they act as hidden advertising for goods sold in the shops. Popular cartoon series such as *My Little Pony, Care Bears* and *Thundercats* fall into this category.

Children and advertising

So alarmed have some people been at this development during the late 1980s that groups were formed to alert public attention to it. In the USA, a group called Action For Children's Television (ACT) was set up to campaign for high quality children's television programmes. They were against the toy-based programmes, fearing that their low cost would enable them to take over programming for children. In the programmes themselves, however, they found little cause for complaint. A British version of ACT has been established and one of its founding members argues:

> It is not gullible for little children to like Care Bears – attractive and comforting (if somewhat expensive) toys; it is perfectly normal. The movies . . . are some of the very few examples of full-length feature film entertainment which are suitable and accessible to very young children. As such, they are a perfect godsend to adults, in full possession of their faculties, who want to introduce their children to the pleasures of cinema-going, and are looking for enjoyable ways of spending an afternoon at half term. The difference in quality between *The Care Bear Movie* and *My Little Pony* was an interesting talking point between me and Elinor [the writer's small daughter] – she, too, enjoyed the first more than the second and we were able to identify a number of reasons why this was so. We did not feel any desire to add to our collection of Care Bears and My Little Ponies – a collection which has provided some enjoyable hours of play in its time – as a result of seeing the movies. (Maire Messenger Davies, *Television is Good for Your Kids*, 1989.)

1 Do you think children need special protection from advertising?
2 Do you think this should apply to all advertising or just to certain types?

Benetton target their clothes at children as well as adults.

43

Conclusion

Some defences of advertising by people sympathetic to the advertising industry can be seen as superficial or self-interested. Likewise, some attacks on advertising seem to come from the reflex actions of critics opposed to advertising because of its connections with a competitive capitalist economy. This book has tried to introduce you to these arguments, and also to help you explore some of their nuances and complexities.

The most recent argument about advertising is a reaction to the extremes of this debate: concern is voiced for the unequal relation between advertiser and consumer. Not too much anxiety, however, is felt for the advertising itself. Indeed, these critics appear to enjoy much of what advertising agencies produce. Still others argue against the historical debate about advertising. They believe that it pays too little attention to the power of ordinary people to use advertising for their own purposes, and not just as consumers.

This most recent aspect of the debate about advertising pays much more attention to what people actually use advertising for. This may be one of the ways to develop our understanding of advertising. Whatever the advertising industry thinks advertising is for, and whatever critics fear advertising might be doing to people,

Advertising is not only used to promote our material needs. This still is taken from a cinema advert made for The Samaritans, an organization set up to help people who feel that life has become too much for them to cope with.

Advertisers know that we all look forward to international harmony. This advertisement made by Saatchi & Saatchi for British Airways involved the aerial filming of over 4,000 children taken from many different cultures. It is an open question, however, whether advertisers reflect such dreams of unity or exploit them.

it is important to have faith in people's control of their own uses of and reactions to advertising. In this way the argument is widened and does not simply revolve around simple support for or opposition to advertising. One of the proponents of this argument provides the final quotation in this book:

> We know a great deal about the content of advertising messages and something about how children perceive and understand this content. But what they actually do after receiving the message is a different matter again. What evidence there is suggests that both parents and children tend to do what they want to do — and that advertising may reinforce them in their decisions. One of the great strengths of the human mind is its power of refusal. It can learn to understand every nuance of meaning, both explicit and implicit, in a persuasive message; it can be emotionally moved by the message; it can swear blind it will obey the message. And, at the end of the day, it can still reject it. Although the sheer weight, volume and sophistication of commercial propaganda may be worrying, we should be reassured by the fact that one of the first words learned by human children everywhere is 'No'. (Maire Messenger Davies, *Television is Good for Your Kids*, 1989.)

Are you reassured? How much attention should be paid to what people do with advertising? How important is the power of advertising and the advertising industry? Are concerns about this power misplaced? Or is 'the sheer weight, volume and sophistication of commercial propaganda' still a cause for continuing debate?

Future markets
Saatchi & Saatchi were among the first advertising agencies to work towards the idea of 'globalization'. They see the world as one great market, with giant corporations selling the same product and using the same strategy and advertising agency in all their markets.

Glossary

Advertising agency A company which organizes advertising campaigns to sell products for different companies.

Advertising industry Consists of companies which advertise, agencies which devise advertising campaigns and authorities which regulate advertising activities.

Capitalism An economic system based on the private ownership of the means to create jobs and wealth; most western societies are capitalist.

Commerce The activity of buying and selling goods.

Consumer A person who buys or whom advertisers intend should buy advertised products.

Copy Material that has been written for an advertisement.

Corporate In commerce, manufacturers combining in a group for a greater share of the market for their product.

Criticism The business of analysing and judging.

Culture The shared system of beliefs, ideas, relationships and activities that identify any group of people eg national, business and youth cultures.

Debate A discussion in which opposing arguments are heard.

Feminist criticism Analysis from women's points of view.

Free enterprise The belief that businesses should be free to compete without control by government and the state.

Graffiti Writing over another's messages, often to deface the original intention.

Learning curve The time it takes a consumer to learn what is being advertised in a new campaign.

Manipulation The idea that adverts persuade consumers to buy products in hidden ways.

Market Any place where buying and selling of goods occurs.

Market research Investigation into what consumers do with advertising.

Mass People as a large group rather than individuals.

Mass consumption The purchase of goods on a large scale.

Mass production The production of goods on a large scale.

Materialism The acquisition of goods, property and wealth for its own sake rather than for need.

Medium Radio, television or print; known collectively as the media.

Product An item of goods which is advertised for sale eg a tin of beans.

Profit The sum of money left over from the sale of a product after its manufacturing and marketing costs have been deducted.

Propaganda Any activity that spreads particular opinions or ideas.

Psychoanalysis The science of how the unconscious mind works.

Psychology The science of how the human mind works.

Racism The belief that some ethnic groups (commonly white) are inherently superior to others (commonly black).

Sexism The belief that one gender (commonly male) is inherently superior to another (commonly female).

Social sciences Disciplines which study social and human arrangements.

Socio-economic system The social and economic arrangement of a society.

Sponsorship Paying for or towards the costs of an event such as a sports meeting or television programme.

Stereotype The act of reducing complex traits into simple ones eg thinking of women as only wives and mothers.

Unequal relations Relations in which one person or group has more power to act than another.

Further Information

You can contact these organizations for posters, leaflets and more details about the operation and regulation of the advertising industry.

In the UK

Advertising Association (AA)
Abford House
15 Wilton Road,
London
SWIV INJ

Advertising Standards Authority (ASA)
Brook House
2–16 Torrington Place
London
WCIE 7HN

In the United States

American Advertising Federation
1400 K Street
North West Suite 1000
Washington DC 20005

In Australia

Advertising Standards Council
St Andrews House
Sydney Square
NSW 2000

In Canada

Canadian Advertising Foundation
350 Bloor Street East
Toronto
Ontario
M4W IH4

Further Reading

Torin Douglas, *The Complete Guide to Advertising* (Macmillan, 1985)
Gillian Dyer, *Advertising as Communication* (Methuen, 1982)
Erving Goffman, *Gender Advertisements* (Macmillan, 1979)
Sally Henderson and Robert Landau, *Billboard Art* (Angus and Robertson, 1981)
Brian Henry (editor), *British Television Advertising: The First 30 Years* (Century Benham, 1986)
David Lusted, *Advertising* (Wayland, 1988)
Kathy Myers, *Understains* (Comedia, 1986)
David Ogilvey, *Ogilvey on Advertising* (Pan, 1983)
Jill Posner, *Spray it Loud* (Routledge and Kegan Paul, 1982)
E S Turner, *The Shocking History of Advertising* (Penguin, 1952)

For teachers
Len Masterman, *Teaching the Media* (Comedia, 1985)
BFI Education, *Selling Pictures, 1983* (BFI Publishing, 21 Stephen Street, London WIP IPL)

Picture acknowledgements
Abbott, Mead & Vickers (RSPCA) 8; Advertising Standards Authority 28, (Paul Seheult) 40; Benetton 6 (top), 43;BMP DDB Needham (American Airlines) (top) 5, (Multiple Sclerosis Society) 10, (Spanish Tourist Board) (left) 12; Chapel Studios 18, 33, 40; Eye Ubiquitous (Paul Seheult) 14, (R Friend) 19, (Tony Honess) 24, (Helen A Lisher) 35, (VC Sievey) 39; Format (Brenda Prince) 37; John Frost Historical Newspaper Service (Paul Seheult) 16; Howell Henry Chadlecott Lury 27; Hutchison 13 (Nick Hadfield) 20; Labour Party 26; © 1990 Marvel Comics 41; Mark Power (bottom) 6; Rex 23; Saatchi & Saatchi (Anchor) 11, (British Rail) (right) 12, 21, (The Samaritans) 44, (British Airways) 45; Paul Seheult 38, 42; Topham 4, 15, 29, 31, 34; Wayland Picture Library 5 (bottom), 7, 9, 17, 22, 25, 28, 30, 32; Zefa 36. The cover illustration is by Andrew Bunday.

Index

Page numbers in **bold** may refer to both illustrations and text. Others refer to text alone.

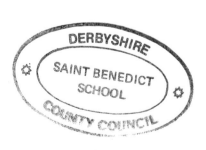